I0486187

Resume Hacks
Creating a Powerful & Engaging Resume that Gets Results!

By

David Peters

Disclaimer

This publication is designed to be used a resource only and not as a definitive plan or approach for any specific resume or opportunity. Every situation is different and some or all parts of this book might or might not apply. For that reason the writers, distributors and publishers of this book assume no responsibility for any or all parts of this book. It is the sole responsibility of the reader to decide the suitability of use or application of any and all parts of this publication.

Contents

Introduction

If you want to get your first job or your next great job, you are probably going to have to create a resume as part of the application process. That resume can take many forms from a simple one-page typed or printed document to an online version submitted through an online process. Whatever form you use, the purpose of the resume is pretty much the same. It allows people to get a bit of insight into who you are as both a person and as an applicant.

Resumes have evolved over time from a simple or generic objective followed by your education and experience. Employers are becoming more discerning, the pool of potential applicants is much larger with the creation of the internet and there are just more and more technological factors that have changed the entire process.

So I guess you could say that the bad part is that there are more applicants for every position but the good part is that the average applicant has so many more opportunities to explore and apply for. An added bonus is that with almost everyone having a computer, or at least access to one, the resume creation process can be so much easier today than it was 30 years ago.

In fact, the approach we are going to discuss in this book is so easy to do today that there really is no excuse for not following it. But this same approach, that is so easy today, would have been a LOT more difficult before computers were so common. So again, this is good news and the entire process will be so easy that you will probably not find a single reason why you can't follow it.

Before we get started, I want to make one thing very clear to everyone reading this book. Creating an exceptional resume is a process and the process takes time. It is an easy process and well within the abilities of almost everyone and even if it isn't for some reason, there are people who can help you along the way.

But even though it is a process once the process has been gone through it is very easy to maintain and update as new jobs become available or new opportunities arise. You are not going to have to start over from square one. The beauty of this process is that you will be able to make changes on the fly and be ready to respond quickly to whatever opportunity might come your way.

So go through the process and take your time. The work you do now will help you not only for the job you are applying for today but also the ones you might be applying to next month or next year. Everything comes through the process and the results you get tomorrow will come about through the efforts you put in today.

The Purpose of the Resume

As with anything you are writing, it is important that you understand the purpose or intended function of the document so you can choose the right approach, wording and content. You wouldn't start a conversation with someone without knowing why you wanted to talk to them or what you wanted to talk to them about so we should approach writing in pretty much the same manner.

Most people think that a resume is just an outline or synopsis of your qualification for a specific job or any job that is available at a certain company. While that is certainly one way to look at a resume, there is another, far more useful, way of looking at this document.

Consider your resume an introduction of you and all the features and benefits that you have to offer.

It is a "sales sheet" and you are the product that you are trying to sell. This document's primary function is to get the person reading it to want to know more about you and invite you in for an interview. It is not intended to get you a job. It is intended to get your foot in the door.

The harsh reality is that there are a LOT of applicants for most desirable jobs these days. Companies post their job on more and more recruitment and job sites instead of going to just one recruiter. So whereas you might have had 15 applicants for a position 20 years ago, you might have 1,500 applicants for that same type position today.

Because a company cannot interview 1,500 applicants in person because it would be too time consuming and too costly, they use resumes and cover letters to identify those candidates that appear to be good matches for a given position. If your qualification and experience are interesting and appropriate, you stand a good chance of getting in for that first interview.

So your resume, is going to be a highly condensed sales sheet listing the most powerful and strongest features and benefits that you have to offer. The single most important purpose of your resume is to make you look like the most perfect candidate for the position you are applying for. It must also communicate an honest commitment on your part for that position.

It needs to be specific and it needs to set you apart from everyone else that submits his or her own resume.

Just like a customer might look at 10 different types of cars before they make their selection, the Human Resource person or the person doing the hiring is going to want to see several

Always remember the real purpose of the resume as you create it. Remember that the resume is an introduction and should be designed, written and crafted with just one purpose and intention in mind. That is to get you to the next level in the process. That might be an in-person or telephone interview or whatever the next step might be. But that is what the resume is used for. To get you to the next step in the process.

So as you design and write your resume, remember what your ultimate goal is for this document. Choose every word and phrase with that goal in mind. Don't just write down the first thing that pops into your head and leave it at that. Think of yourself as a product and figure out how to best convince the person reading it to "buy" you instead of someone else.

The Purpose of the Cover Letter

When you send a resume in to a company by regular mail, you usually send an introductory letter, called a cover letter, with the resume as well. If you send your resume by e-mail your cover letter might also be in the form of an e-mail with the resume as an attachment. Whatever form your cover letter might be in, the purpose is the same.

Your cover letter is designer to let the person reading it understand what job you are applying for, why you want it and why you would be such a great fit for the position. It is a more personal document where you can allow some of your personality and other things about you shine through.

Here is where you can start showing them that not only are you impressive as far as education and experience are concerned but also as a reputable and responsible person as well.

It is sometimes difficult to understand which is seen first, the cover letter or the resume. Since many applicants might be applying for the same job and time is limited for scanning and reading resumes, you might have either resume or cover letter read first. That means that BOTH the resume AND cover letter should be well crafted and impressive. Because if one isn't impressive the other might never get seen at all!

Most, if not all, of what we are going to discuss about resumes will also apply to cover letters as well. So as you go through this book try and determine or at least think about how to apply the concept or topic to both resume and cover letter. Your end goal should be to have professional and effective looking copies of both.

One common mistake many people make is that they have 500 resumes printed up and then create a customer cover letter for each job they apply for. The problem with this approach is that BOTH the resume and cover letter should be customized for the particular job you are applying for. Interviewers and other professionals can spot a form letter or generic resume a mile away and are more likely to cast them aside than a custom one.

As far as length is concerned I believe a one-page cover letter is usually sufficient when combined with a well-crafted resume. In those cases both documents work together. Whatever might not fit into a resume, or even necessarily belong in the resume, can often be included in a cover letter. This allows the applicant to get more information to the interviewer or screener without having long and boring documents.

Make sure the cover letter has all your contact information on it in case that it gets separated from your resume and that you specifically mention the position you are applying for. Very often there will be multiple positions open at the same time and listing it in your cover letter will let the company know which one you are interested in.

Don't make people guess or assume anything at this point. You want them to know what you are applying for, why you think you are perfect for the job and what qualifications and experience you feel are the most relevant.

Also keep in mind that you must capture the interest of the reader as soon as possible when it comes to your cover letter. So be clear and straight to the point and let them know as soon as possible why you are the perfect candidate for the position. Don't make them make the connections between your experience and how it applies to this job.

Lead them through all the connections so they see the whole picture.

Every word, every phrase and every line in your letter should advance your candidacy in the eyes of the person reading it. If it doesn't accomplish that then you should rewrite the line using different wording or phrasing or consider eliminating the line altogether. Like any good advertisement, it should capture the attention of the viewer or reader and build a compelling argument for choosing you over anyone else!

As with your resumes, don't use really small fonts in order to cram more content into one page. I would think 12pt. fonts are the best. Larger fonts look too big and might give the impression that you are using larger fonts to take up more space on the page because you don't have enough good content to fill the page when normal size fonts are used. Smaller fonts might be harder to read especially someone with less than perfect vision. You don't want to have your letter or document discarded because someone couldn't easily read it. So keep the fonts around 12 pt. so the document looks nice and is easy to read.

Leave room at the end for a hand written signature (if hard copy) so the letter has a more personal feel to it. You do not want anyone to think that this is the same cover letter you have sent to 100 different companies for 100 different jobs.

Show the reader that you took the time and made the effort to create a powerful and well-crafted cover letter just for them. Our process will take a LOT of the work out of this but no one will have to know that but you!

Design & Format

How your resume looks is just as important, possibly even more important, than the content in the resume itself. Not because your experience or education isn't top notch but because a professional, great looking resume will make the reader think positively about you even before he or she reads a single word.

If your resume is ugly or messy or looks like a Kindergarten Mother's Day card, people will think that you either lack basic writing and formatting knowledge or that you just didn't care enough about the opportunity to spend the time and effort creating something that looked good. Either way this is not the impression you want to give the person who is deciding whether you go any further in the evaluation process.

The good news is that creating a great looking, professional resume is not difficult. Modern word processors make this easy. All you need to know is a few easy things to become aware of.

Even if you don't want to create something yourself you can use a template available within the word processor or from a third-party website that sells resume supplies and assistance. In other words, there is absolutely no reason why you should not be able to create an amazing resume by the time you are finished.

Assuming you are going to create your own resume, here are a few things that you should be aware of that will help make your resume look professional and be easy to read:

Make it Clear

Your resume should be easy to understand. It should be printed on a good printer that produces clear and sharp characters. This is not the job for a $39 printer from the 1990's! If you have a good quality printer then print it at home. Otherwise, take the digital file to a local copy center and have them print your resume. Cheap printers, like using cheap paper, indicate a lack of professionalism.

Make it Easy to Read

Creating a resume that is easy to read includes a few different things.

First, the fonts should be large enough for the average person to read easily and without much effort.

Keep in mind that yours will be just one of many resumes and if the reader cannot read it easily they could just toss it aside and move on to the next one. A good font is 12 as smaller fonts tend to be harder to read and larger fonts just look out of place on a resume.

Use words that people are far more likely to understand and comprehend. A resume is meant to be read and understood not be an opportunity to show off your impressive vocabulary skills. If someone has to take out a dictionary to go through your resume, don't expect to get much further in the process. You will not impress the person, you will frustrate them instead.

Use Wide Margins

Just because a sheet of paper is 8.5 X 11 does not mean you can or should cram your resume into every bit of space. Use wide margins on both sides to give your resume a professional appearance. Start at 1" and go from there and settle on what looks good for you. At the top and bottom you should also have margins as well. Most word processors will automatically set the top margin and you can manually select the bottom margin according to what looks good and the formatting of the text.

Not only do margins make the document look professional but they also give people space to write notes or other information during an interview or throughout the evaluation process.

This helps the interviewer keep notes straight and all on one sheet of paper so they can easily follow the resume throughout the process.

Have plenty or "White Space"

White space refers to the area of the paper that does not contain any printing. Having the appropriate amount of white space tends to make the document look and flow better and makes it easier and more pleasing to read. Trying to cram too much into too little space can make the document appear crowded.

Examples of white space are the area in your margins, space between sections of the resume and any other area where printing does not occur. You can increase white space by carefully designing your sentences to say more in less space. Make sure your document appears organized and has an "open" type of feel to it and is not too crowded.

Above & Below the Fold

In advertising, material "above the fold" refers to the content that is on the upper half of the page. Since most people read from the top down, it stands to reason that the material on the upper half of the page will be read more often than the material on the bottom half of the page.

That is because people will continue to read only if they feel the material relates somehow to them or their lives and that they feel the material has value to them. If they become bored or disinterested, they are likely to stop reading and go to something else.

When it comes to resumes, the average time people spend initially reading the resume is between 5-10 seconds. If you do not capture the interest and attention of the reader within that time frame, your resume might be discarded without being fully read. To avoid this happening to your resume, you need to have interesting and compelling content on the upper half of the page.

This means that you should pay special attention to the content and the choice of wording on the upper most portion of the page. While content everywhere is important, you MUST make the upper half of the page "jump out" at the reader and capture their interest. One very important part of the upper page is the Objective or Career Summary section which is almost always near the top. Creating an attractive and compelling career summary can get people interested in your really fast if that statement is worded carefully.

Keep in mind that every line of your resume should be designed to make the reader want to read the next line. This should continue throughout the entire resume so that the reader stays engaged and continues to read.

Once you lose the attention of the reader you run the risk of everything that follows never being seen at all no matter how impressive or amazing it might be.

Remember this: What is never read, never matters.

Reverse Chronological

Resumes should always be designed with the most recent events listed first. So your current job would be listed first followed by your previous job and then the job before that and so on. The same applies for your education history. Most recent first and then work backwards.

This is because your highest level achievements and responsibilities are usually among your most recent ones. Interviewers want to know what you are doing now and what you have accomplished now. They do not want to slog through what you did 20 or 30 years ago since that might not even be relevant any more.

Experience First, Education Second

Unless you graduated from an extremely prestigious university and were valedictorian or had some other amazing achievement, your interviewer is likely to be more interested in your experience and accomplishments rather than your education.

Experience is more important because it indicates what you are capable of instead of just your intelligence.

Companies look for college grads not so much because their mastery or 18th Century Literature will enable them to compete in the business world but because completing a college level curriculum indicates that you have at least a certain level of intelligence. This indicates that you have the ability to learn new things that the company needs to teach you. So your education indicates how likely you are to be able to do something in the future while your experience indicates what you have already done. This is why experience will sometimes enable someone to get a better job even though they might not meet the educational requirements.

Universal Readability

You can have the best looking and most awesome and powerful resume ever designed or created but it will do you no good if the person you send it to can't read it. Or, if the resume they see looks different from the resume you created. This can easily happen today when you submit your resume via e-mail or through an electronic submission.

Because of this you should understand that not everyone has the same programs on their computer than you do.

Whenever a different program is used to view an electronic document the formatting and overall appearance can change dramatically. What looked great on your screen might look horrible on someone else's.

For this reason make sure that you send your resume in an appropriate format. If you own the latest word processing program do not save it in the latest format. If the person reading it has an older version it might not read the file you sent them at all. Even if it does, the formatting can change. Save the document in an older version to help insure compatibility.

Personally, I prefer creating a document and saving it as an Adobe PDF file and sending that instead. Sending it as a PDF file almost insures that it will look exactly as you intended it to look. Just about everyone has a PDF reader on their computer and all companies have them as well. There are just too many documents out there in PDF format to be without it.

Keep in mind as you create your resume that it must look professional and be easy to read. I don't mean to keep repeating myself when it comes to this but if someone can't read it easily they are more apt to toss it in the wastebasket instead of reading further. Creating your resume is a results oriented process.

What that means is that everything we do is measure by whether or not we get the job. Having our resume read all the way through is a most important first step.

Proper Length of a Resume & Cover Letter

Remember a few pages back when we said that the average time spent initially looking at a resume was somewhere between 5 and 10 seconds? Well that means that your resume must be able to convey the most important information in just a few seconds or you might allow an opportunity to slip right through your fingers!

Most resumes should be at most 2 pages long. If you can convey everything in one page, that's even better. But for most people with considerable experience and work history, two pages should be your limit. If it is any longer it might be dismissed outright because the person in charge of going through all the resumes just doesn't have the time to read your great novella.

Also, do not think that you can just make the paper larger in order to keep to the two page limit. Resumes should be on standard letter size paper unless specified differently. Do not submit a legal size resume as this might not be able to be scanned or processed. This alone might disqualify you from consideration.

Cover letters should be no more than one page long for pretty much the same reasons. You do not want your letter to be so long that no one is going to bother to read all the way through just to get a few pieces of information. Keep it short and sweet and include only the most impressive and relevant information in your cover letter. Details and other information can be given in an interview.

Resumes and cover letters are perfect examples that the old say "less is often more" is completely true. If you can provide all the important information in one page, don't take 10 pages to do it. If you can say something in one sentence, don't take 5 sentences to say it. People just do not have the time to go through a lot of seemingly worthless text to get what they want.

In the pages that follow we will discuss how to write the most effective resume. We will discuss word choices and format and several other things. But as you go through all of that, keep the one and two page limits in mind and do not exceed them. If you try to say too much to the person reading it, you might wind up saying nothing at all.

The possible exception to this rule is when you are applying for a very high level position that requires a lot of experience, education and achievements. Though these jobs represent a miniscule percentage of the jobs most people apply for, these jobs might require resumes that are a bit longer.

For resumes that are sent in online using a pre-designed template from the website, keep in mind that the same rules for reading often apply. Do not max out every section as far as characters are concerned. Follow the same processes as far as condensing information and keeping it under the equivalent of two printed pages.

But also keep in mind that there are other ways to provide information other than a resume and cover letter and we will discuss those as well. There are many ways to get your information out in front of people other than your resume or cover letter. So keep these limits in mind as you proceed.

Connecting All the Dots!

Many of us who write resumes think for granted that the reader is going to see the relevancy of everything in our resume as they read it. That can cause problems on several levels and might cause you to not have important information appreciated or recognized. If you want to get the most out of your resume, make an effort to connect all the dots and be able to lead the reader through all the connections and relevancies.

Sometimes the people reading the resumes might not be the ones doing the actual hiring or have the required knowledge or expertise to understand everything about the job. Instead they are given a list of qualifications and they scan through the resumes for people meeting those qualifications. But if there is something in your resumes that is directly relevant and important and you do not point that out, it might go totally unnoticed and hurt your overall candidacy.

Sometimes the process goes through several different levels and by not explaining or pointing out the relevance of everything in your resume you run the risk of any one of the people engaged in the process not fully understanding the importance of whatever they are reading. That could either hurt your chances or get your resume tossed early on just because no one realized how important your experience really was.

As we explain our education and work experience, we need to tell a story about what we have done and why it is so relevant. Some people list the particular qualification and then their experience that is relevant to that qualification. Other people word things differently and tie the item with the relevancy all in one line.

However you manage to do it, tie everything together and have your resume tell a story about you, your experience and how it directly related to the job you are applying for. Do not just list what you've done, explain how what you have already done will help in in this new position. Don't leave any room for assumptions or guesswork. Instead, lay it all out in front of them in your cover letter and resume.

Then, as the process moves forward carry on this same approach to your interviews as well.

Make everything neat and organized so they can easily see why your experience is so relevant and why you are the best person for the job. Sometimes when you leave others to connect the dots, those dots are never connected or connected wrong.

Targeted vs.
Untargeted Resumes

There are several different formats and designs of resumes but for this chapter, we are going to talk about resume types. There are two very basic types of resumes people send out to prospective employers. Those two types are targeted resumes and untargeted resumes. They might look the same on the surface but in reality only one of those resumes is really effective when it comes to impressing the person reading it.

Untargeted resumes are those resumes that we create and then print in bulk and send to anyone posting a job opening regardless of what that job might be and regardless of the qualifications. These resumes are not specific at all and are just mass produced to allow us to respond to the most job offerings as possible in the shortest period of time.

And they are generally very poor performers in terms of the results they get. I would try and find a situation where these are the best resumes to use but the only possible one I could come up with is where you hear about a job where you have to get a resume out within minutes to avoid missing a deadline. I cannot think of any other possible situation where sending out a generic e-mail is the way to go.

Think of the message you are sending someone when you send a generic or untargeted resume. You are basically telling them, "I wanted to apply for the job not so much that I was willing to spend 15 minutes fine tuning my resume for this job. So just take this generic one and give me a call. If it is not too inconvenient maybe I will come in for an interview." Though this might not be your attitude or intention that could be the message you are sending prospective employers.

So unless you have only minutes to respond to a job posting or offer, never send a generic or untargeted resume to anyone for any reason. Not only are they unlikely to get a positive result, they will be spotted for what they really are by most seasoned resume evaluators. You are much, much better off sending out targeted resumes which almost always get better results.

Targeted resumes are resumes designed and created for a particular or specific job. They are written and words chosen for a specific situation or job and those words are chosen for maximum effect and maximum relevance.

In other words, if you are applying for a job as a project manager, EVERY word or phrase used in that resume should make you appear a stronger candidate for a project manager position.

Targeted resumes allow you to include much more relevant information for the job you are applying for. They allow you to target specific experience or education and help highlight specific things you have done that will showcase your project management abilities and successes.

In a targeted resume you can pick and choose specific items that will make you look better in the eyes of the reviewer while leaving out any other items that might not be relevant. The end result is a resume that is optimized for one specific job and makes you look the most favorable and skilled for that job. It also helps send the right message to the reviewer of the resumes.

A targeted resume tells the reviewer that you cared enough to take the time and effort to create a customized and targeted resume for this one job or opportunity. It shows the reviewer that you gave this some thought and that applying for this job was important to you. It also tells them that this resume was not part of a "shotgun blast" of 100 resumes to see which jobs you would get a call back on.

Since most companies do not want to waste time on candidates who really don't care about the job, a custom and targeted resume will always get more favorable attention than an untargeted one.

Targeted resumes actually allow you to create a resume and cover letter that showcase your own qualifications and experience by taking what the company is actually looking for and using that same verbiage in your cover letter. For example, if the job posting mentions "at least 5 years of project management experience" you can put this in your cover letter: "My 11 years of high level project management has enabled me to use my management and organizational skills to bring every project in one time and under budget."

Doesn't that sound more impressive while adding a little bit of extra information that will capture the interest of the person reading the resume? Doesn't that statement make you look like a better candidate while connecting the dots a bit more by highlighting your experience in bringing project in on time and under budget?

It used to be that resumes were hand typed and printed in bulk and back then before computers you could make an argument for doing that and sending them out. But today with everyone having access to a computer, you can easily create a master resume and then change bits and pieces around to make a custom targeted resume.

In some cases you can create a targeted resume in less than 30 minutes! Then you save it and possibly use it later on another job posting making just a couple of minor changes! The entire process is quick, simple and extremely effective. You can send out targeted resumes or you can take the lazy way out and send the generic ones. Just be prepared to wait longer for that call from prospective employers. That is because they will call all the targeted resumes first before they even think of calling you!

E-mail, Paper & Electronic Formats

I must preface this chapter by saying that I grew up in the paper and mailing of resumes which was before the digital age and online submission. But over the years while some things have changed other things remain pretty much the same. Resume creation is one of them. We might deliver them differently but the information we include has stayed pretty much the same over the years. In fact, a resume I created 30 years ago today would still work very well.

I always preferred paper resumes as they could be passed around easily, shared with other people around the table and general copied and distributed to whomever might have the need to see it. But the reality is that through e-mail and other electronic services this could be done via e-mail as well. Sometimes, especially when company offices are scattered about, sometimes sharing by e-mail is much easier.

I would advise anyone looking to get a job that they are really interested in to subject their resume in all of the appropriate formats. If the company wants it submitted via e-mail, then send it via e-mail. If you have a particular person to e-mail it to, send it to that person but then also send a hard copy to that person as well.

This can be beneficial in that sending both e-mail and hard copy versions will put your name and resume in front of the same person at least two times. They will see it in their e-mail and they will see it later when the hard copy arrives. They might not remember you but the name will sound familiar. This could result in more of your resume actually being read. When the person realizes you also sent in an e-mail copy this will show initiative and commitment on your part as well. However, if the posting or ad specifically says not to submit hard copy versions then respect their wishes and no not mail out the hard copy.

Another reason for sending out the hard copy is that often times we do not know if our e-mail was actually delivered or not. Unless there is a generated message telling us it was received we just have to hope and pray that it did. By sending the hard copy as well we give ourselves a second chance that the person who needs to see our resume will actually get to see it.

You might even preface your cover letter by letting them know this is a follow-up submission to insure that the e-mail was received.

Hard copies are also less likely to be accidently deleted or placed in the trash by hitting the wrong button. But the main reason is to just get your resume one additional chance to get looked at. Sometimes the reviewer has a certain set of expectations starting in and after looking at all the resumes they realize they need to reduce their expectations. But your resume has already been looked at and they might not go back to it. That hard copy that shows up a few days later may have new life to it.

As we said before, your resume should be created in such a way that the person seeing it is seeing the same document you created and formatted. To eliminate most formatting in compatibilities and other issues, try and save your resume as a PDF document unless the website specifies an alternative format. PDFs almost always look that same whenever they are viewed and this will insure your resume looks good to all who read it.

PDF files can easily be attached to e-mail. In that case the resume is seen as an attachment and the e-mail itself becomes your cover letter. The purpose of the e-mail is to create interest enough for the reader to want to open the resume. From that point on the resume takes over and starts building your case for an invitation for an interview.

The great thing is that with most word processors today you can save a file in almost any different format. So when you get done with your resume you can save it as a word document, a PDF, a picture format such as a JEPEG or anything else that might be required. There usually is not need to create a new resume for a certain format. Just use the drop down box when you hit save to see what options you have at your fingertips.

As far as creating a PDF is concerned you might not have that ability. But there are several PDF creation programs out there and they are not that expensive. They can really come in handy if you frequently have to print things out for others. PDF format is as close to a universal format as you can get so having the ability to save under that format is a great thing to have.

Using Keywords

It might surprise a few of you that sometimes our resumes are not actually read at all. Instead they are scanned into an evaluation program that looks for certain words and phrases that pertain to the position being applied for. If those words and phrases happen to be included in your resume you may get picked for an interview or at least further consideration. If they are not in your resume, then good luck with the next job you might be applying for because you are out of the running for this one.

While this is faster and easier for the company because they do not have to compensate someone for having to look and evaluate resumes, it takes the human element out of the equation and that can sometimes mean that information that is really on the resume might go unnoticed because certain words or phrases aren't used.

It can be somewhat of a black and white process that can send some great candidates into the trash can and some lesser qualified candidates go through. Nothing is perfect but that doesn't mean we don't have to deal with it.

While there might be different criteria for selecting the words or phrases that are being searched for in the process, the usual approach for resume creation is to search the job posting and qualifications and use the same terminology and phrases that are in the listing.

For example, if the qualification list says "Over five years' experience in the industry" you would make sure that exact phrase is somewhere in your resume. If another qualification listed is "be fluent in Spanish and French" you can say something like "I am fluent in Spanish and French as well as 3 other languages. The closer you can match the search terms and words the higher score your resume will get.

Other potential keywords are "action words" that indicate the kind of person you are and your accomplishments. Action words such as "inspired, issues, invested, innovated, introduced, facilitated, fortified, diversified, accomplished" and similar words often will trigger a positive score. Keep in mind that they are looking for people who have done many things and have the ability to continue to do so in the new position.

Care should be taken though to place these words in sentences that make sense and have good grammatical structure. In other words, the words should flow in the sentence and sound like they belong. You do not want your resume to appear to use these words in a spamming function to garner a higher score.

If there are so-called "buzz words" normally associated to a particular position or job function you can try to add those in as well. But whenever you do that make sure they appear to belong and that they fit in. After you write a statement go back and re-read it. If it appears to flow awkwardly or just doesn't sound like it makes sense, then rewrite it or eliminate it altogether.

Other keywords might be common certifications, educational degrees, specific terms for experience and performance and other words normally associated with high performance in any given job.

When it comes to using keywords, keep in mind that your primary focus at this time should be on creating a resume that looks good and reads well. Do not allow keywords to interrupt the flow or make your resume appear less focused. Also, do not just list keywords one after another at the bottom of the resume. This might not be looked upon favorably by the person actually reading it.

Good content that is well written is still your best bet for success when it comes to getting your resumes seen and evaluated. Keywords are just one factor. But designing a resume based solely on keywords with little attention to accurate content will hurt you in the end. Remember that after the electronic "review" your resume will wind up in the hands of an actual person who will then scan over it. If it has good content and good structure you will move forward. If the content is crap and the whole thing written on the basis of keywords, your resume will likely be trashed.

Proof Reading

While this might seem like common sense to a lot of you reading this, you should definitely make sure that before you mail or hit send on your resume that the entire document has been thoroughly proof read. Not just scanned over but thoroughly re-read line by line for spelling and grammar mistakes. You would be shocked at some of the resumes that are sent out by some people. Then they wonder why they never received a call back!

When it comes to proof reading, here are a few suggestions that will help you product an accurate and error free resume:

Spell Check It

Though you should never totally rely on spell check to find all the mistakes, it is a good idea to run it first to clear out all the obvious errors. It might even catch a few that you wouldn't catch yourself. It only takes a few moments to scan through a resume and can make the rest of the process go easier and faster.

Read it Twice

Read things at least twice. The more you read something the more familiar you become with it. What you missed the first time around you might catch the second time. Reading even a two page resume should only take a couple of minutes and it can save you a ton of problems down the road.

Read it Aloud

Sometimes things look just fine on the page but when you actually speak the words they don't sound quite right. The flow might be off, the word choice awkward or the meaning might come through totally different. Read the document aloud and listen to how it sounds and flows. If it sounds good, then check for spelling and punctuation next. If it sounds funny or awkward, change a few words and read it again.

Read it Backwards

Try reading your resume backwards. This enables you to slow things down and look at each word instead of a whole sentence at a time. This is especially useful after you have read it through a few times already. Sometimes you brain might rely from memory instead of what it sees and you might miss a few mistakes.

Have Someone Else Read It

It is always a good idea to have someone else read your resume both for scanning for mistakes but also to give you some feedback on the content and the appearance. We all can stand to listen to the input and suggestions of others. Sometimes people have different viewpoints or opinions and listening to those can lead to word changes or content additions or subtractions.

Last, but certainly not least, check the formatting of the document. Do all the margins look good? Are all the columns or indents in the right place and line up with each other? Are the fonts sized well and are they uniform throughout the document? All of these little things can add up to big problems when they are not corrected.

The last thing you should check is how your resume looks after saving it in the different formats. If you are making a PDF, see how it looks in the final PDF. The same with different formats of documents as well. This is because sometimes different versions of the same file might look different. It is best to find out about this now so we can make certain corrections. Then we just save a different corrected version of the file for that format.

The whole idea is to find mistakes before they are seen by others. While no one is perfect there is no excuse today for sending out a document that has mistakes in it.

Especially something as short as a resume. Entire books might have a typo or two but not a 2 page document. Always remember that your resume is a direct reflection on you and how your resume looks to others is how they see you as well.

The Need for Research

Part of every good resume is some research up front about the company and the position that you are applying for. Part of this preparation is to understand what the company is looking for and how to best provide them with that information in the best possible manner. It will also help you with your cover letter as well as your performance during a live or telephone interview.

The more you learn about the company and what it is looking for, the more you will be able to understand how to best present yourself and your experience. Sometimes it is all in the presentation and knowing what's important to the reader often can make all the difference in the world.

A common interview question might be something like "Tell me what you know about our company." If you sit there are just give them some generic information that everyone knows, that will not be very impressive.

But if you could say something like "Well, I know you employ 12,500 people in 15 offices across the United States and Canada and that you have been in business for 35 years and that your stock has risen every year it has been available" well, that shows you did your homework.

But with your resume, you can sometimes tailor your content and phrasing according to what you know about the company. If it has a reputation for hiring the best and the brightest you can show off your education and advanced degrees. If it is big on volunteering or social engagement, you might find a way to include your volunteer work with Habitat for Humanity. It's all in the knowledge of what the company is looking for and finds important.

Fortunately these days anyone can learn about any company in minutes with just a few clicks of their mouse. Financial data, corporate history and articles of all shapes and sizes can be found by doing a simple search. But always be careful that you make sure the information you receive is accurate. People have a habit of spreading lies and rumors disguised as the truth and this could be very damaging and hurt your chances in an interview. Just take the time to confirm anything you might even consider saying in an interview or on your resume. After all you cannot take back something once you say it or put it in writing.

As you research the company, take particular note on how your experience and skills align with the company and what the company is looking for. Also make note of anything the company looks for or stands for and think about how you compare to what they want in an employee. Not everyone is a perfect fit and you might discover that this is not the company for you or that it might be the perfect match! Either way, it is best to know this now to avoid wasting time and effort.

You might also check for the people you might be interviewing with to learn more about them as well. Information can be a great thing when it comes to impressing someone who is in the position of making decisions about your future! You might even locate the names of other people you might wish to send your resume to as well!

Researching the company you are applying to always makes sense but most people do it after they sent in their resume but before their interview. While this still has benefits it is much better to research before so that you can better fine tune your resume and cover letter to the company you are applying to.

If you don't have the time, or you would like another approach you can always do your research in two steps. First, do some basic research so you can target your resume directly to the company and then after you have been contacted for an interview you can do more in-depth research to help prepare yourself for the interview.

This might save you some time especially when you are applying to more than one company at a time.

You might also find yourself applying for a job and not knowing which company made the posting. This can be quite common on online employment sites where the company does not want to publicize that they are looking for people or to fill a specific job. When this is the case with your, it is not possible to research the actual company but you can still research the industry as a whole or several companies in the area figuring that it should be one of those. This will enable you to target your resume better even though you do not know which company is looking for someone.

Please do not dismiss the idea of doing research thinking that it is not a valuable use of your time. Remember that all resumes are part of a competition where the winner gets the job offer. Anything, and I mean anything, that can make you look better in the eyes of the recruiter or company is never a waste of time. Everyone is doing everything they can to look as good as they can.

Why shouldn't you do the same?

The Writing Approach to an Effective Resume

While you don't need to be a best-selling author to write a great and compelling resume, there are a few things you should be aware of as you write your resume. Always remember that your resume is a direct reflection on you and how it reads will have a great impact on how you are perceived by the person reading it.

Your resume should tell a story about you and your expertise, experience and attitude towards that particular job. Every line on that resume should bring the reader further towards wanting to learn more about you and meet you in person. If the resume does not capture the interest of the person reading it, chances are you will not be invited I for an interview.

Writing a compelling resume is not difficult but it takes a bit of practice. You should use highly descriptive words that help create a vivid and bright picture of you as a candidate.

For example, if you were in charge of a group of people, you might write on your resume "Responsible for 10 people" or you might write "Supervised 10 highly motivated and extremely productive individuals". Both saying pretty much the same thing but one makes it sound much better.

The easiest way to learn how to write an effective resume is to write your content first making sure that you have listed everything that you want to include in the resume and place each item in the right location. Once that is done you can go back and take each item and reword it to make it sound more impressive and more powerful.

Go line by line and change the wording around to make things sound better. After you are done with a section, go back and read it through making sure that it flows well and reads properly. Sometimes using too many powerful or descriptive words will make something appear too "phony" or embellished. Sometimes it is a fine balance between just enough and too much.

You should do the same thing when the entire resume is completed. This is because once every individual section is done and tweaked they all must flow together and lead the reader to the same conclusion and down the same path.

If you find that one section is worded towards a different goal or purpose, you will need to go back and make some more minor changes to improve the flow and the focus.

The resume should also be extremely positive with the focus on what you can do and what you have done. No one is interested in the things you haven't done or are not trained on. What people want to know are the things you already have done and done well and what you are capable of.

To help create a more positive feeling and impression in the mind of the reader we want to make use of only positive words. Stay away from the words can't, won't not and other negative sounding or feeling words. You want to create the most positive and compelling document you possibly can.

Flow is extremely important as well. You want the content of the resume to build as the person reads it. You want to take them from who you are through why you want the job, what has prepared you for this job and what you have done to show you are the right person for the job. It is the same as telling a story.

Telling a story requires a flow that helps connect the different sections of the resumes as the person is reading it. The content of the resume should be answering the questions that come up in the mind of the reader as they are reading it.

For example, your mission statement or objective tells the reader why you want or are interested in the job. The reader might read this and ask themselves "Now I know why this person wants the job but are they prepared for the job?" Then they start reading your education or experience and you tell and show them what you have done or what you have learned that has qualified you for this position.

If you lead with your experience (which you might do if your experience was impressive but your education a bit weak or outdated) and accomplishments, the reader might develop questions about your education which you would answer in the next session. If you lead with your education (which you might do if you education was extremely impressive or your experience was on the weak side)) the reader might say "This person has the knowledge but can they use that knowledge effectively?" Then you would go into your experience and showcase the most impressive and important things you have done that qualify you for the job.

Do you see a pattern here?

A well designed document of any type, including a resume takes the reader from point A all the way through to the end in a well flowing manner. The document tells a story and builds upon itself so the reader is taken down the path we want them to go.

We leave nothing to chance and we connect as many dots as possible.

The document answers the most common questions as they appear in the mind of the reader. Our content can even help form those questions as we write our resume to draw attention towards our strengths and away from our weaknesses. This is not being dishonest or deceptive, it is just making ourselves appear at our very best.

Last, but certainly not least, the reader should be able to understand out style of writing. We have touched on this already and will discuss it more in other chapters but since we are discussing writing styles in this chapter we must also discuss ease of reading as well.

People will read more of something if it is easy to read and follow. So make your resume easy to read by using words that everyone will understand and stay away from technical words or jargon unless you are 100% certain this is going to be read by someone with that particular knowledge. Keep in mind that in most larger companies you resume is going to be read first by a recruiter or Human Resource person who might not know industry jargon or slang.

You should also take care to write on a level that most people feel comfortable reading. For example most newspapers are written at the fifth grade level so they will be understood by most people. You should follow the same approach when writing your resume. You want to make sure whoever reads it, understands it.

As you start creating your resume you will find yourself getting better and better over time as you develop your writing skills and perfect your craft and approach. Just make sure everything flows well and sounds right when you read it aloud. If something sounds wrong or weak, re-write it until you're satisfied.

I would suggest that you give yourself some time before applying for a really big or important job. Develop your resume ahead of time and possibly apply for other position or even just create a resume for apposition you see advertised just so you can get comfortable with the process. You don't have to be perfect when you start out. Your end product is what really matters.

Don't worry about your first draft. No one but you will see it unless you mail it out.

Writing to Your Audience

Another time where research comes in handy is discovering who you will be sending your resume to and who will read it first. This is important because if the first person who reads it doesn't like it or see the value in it going further, no one else will ever get to see it. So your goal is to impress the person reading your resume first in hopes of making it further into the process.

Sometimes you can get a hint or a clue as far as who is going to see your resume by looking at the address you are supposed to submit it to. For example, if the address says "Human Resources" in it your resume is going to go to Human Resources. So you know it is going to stand a good chance of being screened by Human Resources first. If there is a name in the "attention" heading then you know who will see it and you can search under that person's name in the corporate directory or website.

If there is no clue in the address then you will just have to write your resume to what you will have to assume is going to be your audience and that should be the manager of the department or area of the company where you will be working.

Writing to your audience means using words and term that are effective and easily recognizable to whoever is reading your resume. It means creating a document that will resonate with whoever is reading it and make them want to read and learn more about you.

Though every job posting and situation are different, if your resume is going to a Human Resources person or department then you should stay away from extremely technical material, words and jargon and concentrate on accomplishments, education and experience.

If your resume is going to the department that is going to hire you, or if it is going to a specific technically oriented person, you can get more technical and incorporate any words or terms that will impress them with your knowledge and experience. But keep in mind that making it too technical might hurt you if your resume is ever passed on to anyone else.

I always try to write to a specific person but still maintain a resume that can be read and understood by anyone who is reading it.

Even if I know it is going to a technical person I will temper the use of technical words and jargon so the resume will have meaning to others who might read it as well. Don't put all your eggs in one basket or write any resume so that just one person will be able to understand it and appreciate what you have done.

We also should not have to remind you that your audience is going to depend on the particular position you are applying for so that all of you content should specifically related to the job or opportunity you are applying for.

Filter out any content that is not directly relevant or sufficiently impressive when it comes to the position you are applying for. Unless you do not have sufficient directly relevant material leave everything else out. If you still need more material, then pick from your remaining material and choose the most relevant or impressive material to fill out the remaining space.

When you finish everything should point to your ability to excel at this specific job. Not any job in the company but this specific job. The time to show your ability to do other jobs within the company will arrive at your interview. But for now, the entire focus should be on getting called in for that interview and not have your resume tossed in the trash when other resumes look better.

You have heard all of this before earlier in this book and you will hear this again as we move on. You need to do all of this because you will need your resume to be among the very best to even get a shot at that interview. Everyone else is going to be fine-tuning and writing the very best and most impressive and targeted resume they possibly can. Some might even hire professionals to write their resume for them.

If you want your resume to compete with them then you are going to have to take the time required to write in the most effective manner and to the people who are reading it. Remember to always consider the audience your resume, or any other document, is being written for. Then write your resume like you are talking to that person face-to-face.

Many other applicants are doing the exact same thing so you should be doing it as well.

Capturing Interest

The average time someone spends initially reading your resume is going to be about 5-12 seconds depending on how many resumes that person has to go through that day. That means that he or she is not likely to stop and read your resume word for word unless they are given a powerful incentive to do so.

Resume screeners are given one task to do and that is to find the most desirable and highly skilled applicants out of all the resumes that were submitted. But they are usually also given a time limit in which to accomplish that task. They might place a deadline on when the resumes have to be processed by or assign other duties that will limit the amount of time any one person has to go through the resumes.

Add to that the number of resumes they are bound to receive from unqualified people who should not have applied in the first place and you have a lot of resumes and little time to go through them.

Because of this, most resume reviewers are going to skim over or roughly scan the upper parts of your resume to see if there is anything worth a second look.

If the upper part of your resume is boring or does not capture the interest of the reader you run an increased risk of having your resume thrown in the trash as the reviewer moves on to the next one. You might have truly remarkable content and achievements listed further down or on the next page but they will never be seen. And if no one ever sees them, they will not help you get the job.

Think of your resume as a short story. In any short story the beginning of the story is meant to draw the reader in and get them involved in the story. Why? So they keep reading more of the story. If the beginning is boring you are more likely to go to another story or open another book. But if the characters or the plot capture your interest and hold it for a bit, you will read on and get more invested in the story.

The upper part of your resume MUST capture the interest of the reader. It MUST make them want to read more or believe that there is merit in reading more and spending more time reading that resume. You must make the reader feel your resume is worth their time and effort. If you can accomplish that, your resume will be rd. If you can't it won't be read. It really is that simple.

So how can you capture the interest of someone reading your resume for the first time? Here are a few suggestions:

Have a Compelling Objective or Mission Statement

I have seen people use the same generic and ultra-boring objective or statement at the top of their resume. Something like: I am looking for a challenge (boring), I am results driven (more boring) or my favorite I am looking for a challenge (resume is now in the trash, looking for the next one)

Spend some time on your objective or statement and make it unique and directly relevant to the job and the posting itself. If there is something in that posting that is important to the company, work that in and make it important to you. If you accomplished something great and relevant, make sure people see it. Grab their interest and keep it.

Use the Same Words and Terminology as in the Job Posting

If the posting has qualifications in it and you can work them into your objective or opening statement then do it! If the posting says they are looking for a highly educated and experienced person to fill the job make sure they know you fit the bill. Open with something like "Harvard Graduate with Master's Degree and 14 years' experience seeks (then further describe the position you are applying for.)

Make it eye catching and make it what the reader is searching for. The easier and faster they find it, the better off you will be. No generic statements or content here!

Have the Most Relevant Content Early in Your Resume

Everyone has relevant content and not so relevant content in their resumes. Generally speaking the younger you are the more general content you might have because you lack many years of experience. But whether you have 5 years' experience or 50 years, make sure to hit them first with your most impressive and most relevant experience, achievement and qualifications.

The idea is to open their eyes with the most impressive things first so they will stop and look at more of the details. Don't risk boring them with information they might not care about. Hit them quick, hit them hard and impress them within the first few seconds of them reading your resume.

Objective vs. Career Summary

For decades almost every resume had an objective at the top right under the applicants name. This objective was a somewhat generic statement that said what you wanted to be considered for. Sometimes it was very generic and sometimes people actually took a bit of time and created an objective tailored to the specific job they were applying for.

Objectives pretty much accomplished their intended purpose but they were limited in scope as to what they could include and how much they could capture the interest of the reader or prospective employer.

For example the objective: to secure a job in the banking sector utilizing my skills and talents with the chance for advancement" is a pretty generic statement that probably bored the pants off whoever was reading it. The other somewhat valuable piece of information in the entire thing was naming the industry.

Think about that statement for a moment. What did you tell the person who was reading it? You told them you wanted a job. (Duh! Why else would you send in a resume????) You told them what industry you were interested in which hopefully was their industry as well. (Again, DUH!) You also told them you wanted the chance for advancement. (The third DUH, as everyone wants the chance for advancement and larger income!)

So other than fill up a line or two on your resume, that objective pretty much accomplishes nothing except possibly giving the reader one less resume to go through and evaluate. So we need to come up with something different that is more powerful and compelling and gives the reader so more valuable information.

Today, more people are abandoning the objective and instead using something called a "Career Summary." A career summary is more specific, provides more information and allows you to capture the interest of the person reading the resume faster and easier.

Here is an example of a Career Summary:

"A hard working and Dedicated Financial Analyst with 25 years' experience in Private Banking. Works well independently and efficiently and has handled several Fortune 500 accounts. Willing and able to work odd hours and weekends when required."

Now let's take a look at what that tells the person who is reading your resume:

It tells then that you are hardworking which is something everyone likes to hear. It tells them you have 25 years' experience which is a HUGE eye opener especially when looking to fill a higher level position. It tells them you work well without needing to be supervised and also lets them know that your previous accounts were large and important accounts. This lets them know that you were good and your job and trusted to handle these large accounts. It also indicates a willingness and awareness to work odd hours and weekends which might be part of the job as listed in the posting.

Do you see how much better a career summary can be when written properly and effectively? You can include the most important qualification as listed in the job posting and show direct and relevant experience or education to match those qualifications. These will be things that are important to the reader and will make your resume stand out from the rest by capturing the interest of the reader from the very beginning!

Think about that for a moment. If you were the reader and you saw right from the start that someone had 25 years' experience, wouldn't you want to read more? Wouldn't you want to see what else this candidate had to offer? Wouldn't you be snapped out of boredom and be on high alert after reading that?

Of course you would!

By writing a well-constructed and highly tailored career summary you can introduce more information very early into your resume. You can pique someone's interest extremely quickly and set yourself apart from the other candidates. This can be a powerful advantage when it comes to deciding who goes forward and who goes in the trash.

Let me let you in on a little secret that many people are not aware of.

Many jobs don't go to the best possible candidate. Instead, those jobs are given to those who are "perceived" to be the best candidates. That means the person who read the resume developed a highly positive impression early on in the process and that perception carried through until the selection process for interviews. So the people who made the best impression had the best chances of getting that important first interview.

Though qualifications and skills most certainly do matter, so does how you market them and yourself. Take the time to capture the interest of the reader with a compelling and targeted career objective. Use words and terms directly from the job posting to make sure the reader finds you appealing and desirable from the very beginning.

Then your resume will go on the "to be interviewed" pile and not in the circular file.

Creating Your Resume

This chapter is a quick hitter designed to restate a few obvious things while also getting you in the right mindset to write the perfect resume. More than anything this chapter is going to give you a few reasons why you should not take shortcuts and why creating highly targeted or tailored resumes is the only real effective choice you have.

As we already mentioned, getting and interview, let alone a job offer, is a highly competitive process. You are going to be competing with dozen, possibly hundreds of other applicants all trying their best to get an interview. Just like they are doing their best to look their best, you must do the same thing or you will be left behind.

As we get started talking about the individual parts of your resume and how to construct them, you might be tempted to take a short cut or two and use one section over and over again in several resumes.

While you can do this, you are severely limiting the effectiveness of your resume and you also risk losing the attention and interest of the reader.

Chances are your resume is going to be read or screened by people who have read hundreds, possibly thousands, of similar resumes. Because of this they are going to quickly spot a resume that took the applicant 4 minutes to create or even worse, the ultra-generic resume one person sends out for jobs ranging from counter person at a fast food restaurant to mid-level manager.

When someone sees those resumes they immediately come to the conclusion that this person really doesn't care very much for this position and that it isn't very important to them. Now this might be as far from the truth as possible but remember, it is the perception that counts at this point in time. You want to make the reader feel that this job is the single most important focus at this point in time. A generic resume, or even a partially generic one, simply will not cut it.

As we go through the different parts of your resume, there are only two parts of your resume that can be the same. The first part is your name and contact information and the second part, if you even use it, might be your references and even then those should be specific to the job or opportunity as well. So let's play it safe and only duplicate your name and contact information.

Everything else should be different on every resume you send out the door or through your e-mail.

For those of you who think that this is too much work, let me assure you that it is not. It might have been in your parent's day when everything was done on a typewriter. But with today's word processors and computers you can easily pull up existing resumes and fine tune data, cut and paste parts in and move them around and easily change words and phrases to suit your needs.

As you create each new resume and save it under a different name, eventually you will have several different resumes all fine-tuned to a certain type or kind of job. Then when you need that resume, you can open it, make a few minor tweaks and changes and have it ready to go in less than 30 minutes! Even the most last minute opportunity or deadline will allow you to create a custom resume using this process.

That is why it is easier when you start developing your resume earlier. The more different resumes you create the easier it will be to find the right version and make a few small tweaks so that you have a resume that looks like it was created just for this one job. This will make it appear like you are very committed and very serious about the job and the opportunity. In other words, you will stand out from the rest of the pack which should have been your goal all along.

There is only one reason why anyone would send out a generic resume these days. Actually there are two. The first is that they have to send out resumes for some reason or another but don't actually want to land a job. The second reason is that they are just plain lazy. Each way, the generic resume is not likely to land you an interview unless you are going for the really low hanging fruit jobs that no one really wants.

Identify Your Accomplishments

It is frequently said in life that if you do something for someone and need to let them know that you did it, then you did it for the wrong reasons. While this is true for good deeds and helping others out in life, it is certainly not true when it comes to your resume. On your resume, you need to list anything and everything you can accomplished or done in your life or career that is directly relevant to the job you are applying for.

If you accomplished several things that would be seen as important by the hiring company but you don't tell them about it, chances are they will never know and you will not gain any benefit from doing any of those things. Most people have no problem sharing their work history or education but somehow feel that sharing accomplishments or awards is somehow "bragging" about themselves.

Well, let me tell you one important thing. The entire purpose of your resume IS to brag about yourself. Not in a conceited or obnoxious way but to tell everyone what you did, what you accomplished and then tie those accomplishment to the job you are applying for. When you let someone know why things you did are relevant to what they are looking for that is not bragging, it is selling yourself as the most perfect candidate.

Some people feel that the interview is the perfect time to work those accomplishments and experiences into the conversation and you cannot argue with that logic. Interviewer are the perfect time to lead the interviewer through all you have done step by step. There is no disputing that.

But without a compelling and impressive resume that outlines why you have done and what you have accomplished you might never make it as far as getting that interview! You cannot excel or impress someone at step 3 of a process when you never make it to step 2. So you have to do whatever you have to in order to move to the next level. Then worry about what to do then.

I always tell people to keep a running list of their accomplishments and their work history. I also suggest that they also keep a file of praising memos and e-mail and even performance reviews.

All of these things can help you decide which content is the best for any given resume or opportunity. You might have a list of 25 things you did or accomplished but only 5 of them are directly relevant. Keeping a list of everything you have done or are proud of is the single best way to make sure nothing gets forgotten or overlooked and that you always have the best and most specific and relevant information to place in your resume.

The best thing to do is always choose the accomplishments that best suit or fit the job requirements. That way your information can have the most impact in the shortest period of time. If you can match every qualification with an achievement or accomplishment, you will look great to the reader or interviewer. If you can match each item with several accomplishments, that's even better!

Remember what we have said several times already. Other applicants are already matching what they have done and achieved to the jobs they are applying for. If you want to compare favorably you must do the same thing. Choose your content carefully and always go for maximum impact and maximum impression. Don't be obnoxious about it or act conceited but if you did something, let people know about.

Otherwise, you won't get nearly as much benefit from it.

Be Specific

There is another reason why targeted resumes are so much better and that is because they are so much more specific and can impart so much more information in the same amount of space. One thing you can do to make things more specific and more impressive is to use actual numbers and measurement throughout your resume to make people sit up and notice things about you and your experience.

Using numbers and other more specific ways of expressing performance, achievements or values have the effect of making every item more believable and seemingly more real in the process. For example, saying that you came in under budget is nice but saying you came in 6% under budget is more specific and impressive.

For example, here is a common bullet point on a resume:

"Managed the full staff in the procurement office"

OK, that tells the person reading the resume that you had supervisory or management experience and that is important for someone to know. But the statement stops short of providing the full amount of information and the impact the statement might have had.

But what if we changed that statement to:

"Managed a staff of 35 in the procurement office."

This tells the reader that you have supervisory or management experience but it also lets them know the extent of that experience. Managing 35 people is a lot more impressive than managing 2 or 3. It shows a different level of responsibility, organization and workload. The result is a statement that has more impact and looks more impressive.

Anything that you can measure or express in terms of numbers can be enhanced in the same manner. Here are a few examples:

"Graduated from Anytown College with B.S. Degree" could become "Graduated 3rd in my class at Anytown College" This shows enhanced achievement or accomplishment.

"Improved sales in 2015" can be changed to "Improved sales by 21% in the 2015 fiscal year. Without the number increasing sales could have been by .0001% for all the reader knows.

""Created improvements to save resources and improve productivity" can be changed to "Created improvements that saved the company $550,000 while improving productivity on average of 4% per employee." This shows the reader you didn't lower expenses by 25 cents because you purchased a box of paper clips on sale! It shows them real achievements and real gains.

Now as you look at all of these examples, you should have noticed something about each one that was the same. That is that all of the achievements and accomplishments looking were very impressive and the addition of numbers made those accomplishments very specific and impressive.

But you can only do that when what you are talking about is truly impressive or something you should really be proud of. If your accomplishment was very low or very little, then you might not want to use numbers to quantify it because that could work against you.

If you technically made something better or had a tiny accomplishment that you still would like to place in your resume, then consider leaving out the numbers in the hope that the reader will think the accomplishment was great than it really was. This could work in your favor.

But if you did something really great or something you are very proud of, use numbers to make sure people know exactly what you did and are duly impressed. As we have stated already, if you accomplished something great but no one knows about it, you won't get the benefit of it in the evaluation process.

You can mix and match statements that are both generalized and specific in the same resume. But when you do this people might notice the general ones and wonder why these were not quantified as well. This might hurt you a bit but chances are it will not come up unless it is really glaring on the resume.

So go through your resume and see if there is anything you can add specificity to with numbers or any other terminology and go ahead and make those changes. This will help make your resume stand out from the rest and be more impressive and effective. It will also tend to capture more people's attention and hold it longer as well. This will mean that more of your resume gets read and that's almost always a good thing.

Use Bullets Instead of Paragraphs

With a one or two page maximum size and with a lot of information to pack into those pages, we sometimes find ourselves with more information than can get and still look good on a resume. So we need to find ways to get more information into the resume while still making it read well, sound good and look good.

One very good solution that can double, triple or even allow you to fit even more information is to use bullet points instead of paragraphs in your resume. This way each piece of information will take up one line, but definitely less than two lines instead of a paragraph that might take up to 10 lines to adequately describe something in proper grammatical terms.

Here is an example of how you can use bullet points instead of paragraphs:

• Created a new department for handling engineering tasks.

- Brought in every engineering project in under budget
- Responsible for hiring and training new hires.
- Responsible for budgetary performance and expenses on all projects
- Recognized for outstanding achievement 3 times in 5 years.

There are 5 items that fit in less than one quarter of a page because they were short mini sentences listed one right after the other. Notice they are all standalone topics unrelated to each other so each of them would have required a full paragraph of at least 3-5 lines plus the spacing between paragraphs.

Had this same content been expressed in paragraph form it would have taken a full page, possibly more. With a paragraph structure you have to lead into the topic, discuss the topic and exit from the topic. You just cannot have one sentence after another with unrelated content in it. Doing so would make the resume difficult to read and appear disorganized and hap hazard in structure.

The use of bullet points allows you to really hit the reader hard with content as well. With giving the reader one impressive fact or entry after another you constantly are keeping them interested and engaged and are bale to impress them more in less time. This will almost insure that the reader will read through your entire resume.

That is another bonus of using bullet points as well. With the use of bullet points and there shorter allowable structure, you can give the reader a lot more information in the same period of time. Bullet points are much more easily skimmed as well so when the reader is scanning your resume more data and information will be seen and recognized as well.

Bullet points also work well for listing courses taken, achievements, responsibilities and other entries that sometimes are quite numerous. Just make sure that each group of bullet points is under the same overall topic. For example, if you had taken many relevant courses, you can bullet point those courses but do not include an accomplishment within that list of bullet points. Accomplishments would be listed under their own list.

Bullet points really allow you to not only get more information into your resume but make it easier to read and follow at the same time. Bullet points get your information across faster and easier while making it easier to design a good flow throughout the resume as well.

Just remember to keep your bullet points short and sweet. If you expound too much on each item then your bullet points are going to be too long and start resembling paragraphs. Keep them one line or less if possible but two lines maximum for maximum impact, appearance and flow.

Prioritize Every Entry

I always like to create an initial master resume with everything I have done or accomplished and achieved listed in it. With your computer this is easy because you just make lists of everything and then cut and paste them into a master document. Then when you have this master resume, you go back in and delete what doesn't apply and move entries around in order to get the best effect.

Your resume should include the best of the best in everything you know or have done in your career. In other words, you should be listing the strongest, most powerful and most impressive items on your resume at every opportunity. Every entry should be prioritized for maximum effect and maximum impression.

Your master resume might be 6 pages long or more and if it is, that's just fine. But as we take out the little things or remove the non-relevant material, the overall size of the resume will go down.

Ideally we should be looking to get a packed resume down to about two pages. A less packed or entry level resume might be one page.

Regardless of how long your resume might be, make sure to fill the space at first with your most impressive information first and then go down to the next impressive and so on until your resume is the length you feel it should be.

Don't be tempted to use "filler" or weak material just to fill in space. Strong material helps build appositive impression and make you appear to be a better candidate. Weaker material often has the opposite effect. So if something doesn't help your case or make you appear more formidable, then leave it out. The exception to this might be an entry level resume where there is limited content is available.

Eliminate the Obvious

There are a couple of things that used to be done on every resume that just aren't done any more for whatever reason. Things change and one of those changes is the elimination of some information that now seems obvious.

Many resumes in "the old days" had the statement on the bottom "Available for interview" or "References available upon request. Now call me stupid but I cannot figure any possible situation where someone would send a resume in for a job and refuse to come in for an interview. By the same token, I have never heard someone refuse to provide a reference at any point in the hiring process. So both of these statements should not be part of your resume.

Recruiters don't really care about your hobbies or interests either unless they have some direct relevance for the job you are going after.

I guess if you were interviewing for a job with a local charity and one of your hobbies was volunteering with Habitat for Humanity you might want to put that in their somewhere. But otherwise, people really don't care that you collect stamps or spend your weekends bird watching.

Also, if you are in the latter stages of your career or have considerable education and experience people do not need to know which high school you went to and when you graduated. If you graduated from Harvard with a Master's it is assumed you graduated from High School.

Marital status and your overall health condition can be left off as well. Unless either of those has an impact or relevance to the job you are applying for, they should be on no interest. If you are applying for a position as an astronaut, maybe the health issue might be relevant. But you can always confirm your health at your interview.

There may or may not be other things that have no place on your resume as well. Just remember that you want every line on your resume to further your chances for an interview. You want every line to impress and you want every entry to resonate with the person reading the resume. Eliminate everything that does not meet that criteria unless it is a required entry for any specific job.

Connecting the Dots

Do you remember the drawing we used to do as kids where you connected numbered dots on a sheet of paper and as you connected more dots it became clear what the picture was going to be? Well that is exactly the way we have to approach the building of our resume. We have to connect as many dots between our skills and experience and how they apply to the job we are applying for. The more dots we connect the clearer the picture becomes to the person reading our resume.

You and I have an advantage over the person reading our resume. We already know what we do each and every day and how it applies or prepares us for the job we want to apply for. We know our experience is relevant and we know our education enables us to excel in this position. But the person reading the resumes might not know these things.

That is why we need to structure our resume in such a fashion that we take every qualification as it is listing in the job posting and connect it to part of our education, experience or employment history. It is up to us to show the relevance of what we have to offer as it applies to the position we are applying for.

If we don't do this we run the risk of the people reading the resume not making these important connections or seeing the relevance of what we have to offer. That can lead to us not getting the credit or consideration that we should get based on our overall qualifications.

As you create your resume, make a copy of the job posting or qualification list and go down each qualification or requirement and find something relevant in your past history or education and then make those entries in your resume. You want to present yourself as the complete package. The one applicant that has everything you asked for and more.

Don't sit back and wait for them to see how valuable you are and what a perfect fit you might be for the position. Take the initiative and go out and show them. Lead them from line to line and qualification by qualification through your entire resume so by the time they finished that there is no question in their mind that they need to find out more about you.

Leave age or Birthdate Off!

Unless there is a minimum or maximum age component to the job you are applying for, leave that information off your resume. People are not allowed to ask you your age during the interview or employment process and they cannot discriminate against you based on your age either.

But placing that information your resume might be asking for trouble because someone might think you are too young or too old and not allow you to go further in the process. While this is illegal, you will never be able to prove that this took place. There are just too many other reasons and variables that they could say contributed to the decision to exclude you.

So leave it off, make them guess, and get yourself into an interview on your own merits.

Selling Yourself

Keep in mind as you create your resume that you are really creating an advertisement with you as the product you want to sell. Though this might sound a bit crass, it is exactly what a resume is. It is an advertisement designed solely to bring a product (You!) to the attention of the customer (the business or company looking to hire).

Most people do not think of themselves as a product but sometimes it helps to think about yourself in that exact manner so you can look at your resume in another way. When we talk about every entry needing to make the reader feel more and more positive about you as a candidate that is the same as listing features and benefits of a product on an advertisement or sales sheet.

Here are a few other similarities between resumes and advertisements:

They both look to capture the attention of the reader.

They both try to make the product appear a perfect match for what the customer needs.

They both list features, benefits and information about the product.

They both identify a need and attempt to fill that need with the product.

They both compete with other products (people) for the attention of the customer.

So as you develop your resume, ask yourself if it does a good job selling you and all you have to offer. Ask yourself if you would "purchase" or hire you based on what you have read. Does your resume do a great job separating you from the rest of the applicants? Does it make you appear to be the perfect candidate for the job?

Even more important is identifying potential weak spots in you or your resume as well. Every weak spot is a possible negative entry in the eyes of the reader. Since the sales process needs to be as positive as possible to overcome what might be very stiff competition, we need to eliminate, or at least minimize any weaknesses in the text.

Make sure your resume reads like a professional sales letter. Make sure it captures the interest of the reader as quickly as possible and make sure it portrays you, the product, in the best possible manner without lying or being deceptive. The end result should be a strong need to "buy" the product or at least walk into the store (interview) to take a look at it.

Always remember that the sales letter or resume is intended just to get your foot in the door and get you in for an interview. It is not designed to land you a job. That will be up to you later. But for now, in the very beginning, you are going to have to sell yourself just like any other product out there on the shelves.

Once you look at it in this manner, things come into focus a lot faster and a lot easier.

Being Truthful

There is a huge difference between embellishing something and lying. While we should always be looking for ways to make us look better on our resume, the underlying content of the resume must be truthful and not a work of fiction. If your resume has entries that are not true, remove them and re-work that part of the resume. Lying or misrepresenting yourself can cause you a lot of problems now and later even after you have landed the job.

With the arrival of the internet all kinds of information that might have taken hours, days or weeks to gather before can now be obtained in just a few clicks of a mouse or by joining one or two search websites.

What that means is that more and more companies, both large and small, are going to be checking what they find on your resumes. If you say you have a Master's Degree from Harvard you had better have one because they will check.

If you say your address is one address but you actually live somewhere else, they will find that as well. Things such as credit ratings, marital status, sometimes work history and other details about you are all available to anyone who wants to check on them.

Though this can be scary when it comes time for person privacy issues, this does really help you in that it also keeps other from lying about themselves and making them appear to be better or stronger candidates than they really are. But there are a few other reasons we shouldn't lie as well.

Even if the company doesn't find out about certain "errors" on your application if they should find out about them later, you could lose the job you already were given. This has sometimes happened after employment had started and even in cases where people had been employed for years. For most companies this isn't just about lying about experience or education, it is also about personal integrity, honesty and values.

Another reason why we shouldn't lie is that once we do lie we have to live up to that lie. We have to constantly talk as if the lie is the truth. We have to demonstrate abilities based on the education or experience we said we had when we were hired.

Whenever we make statements or provide certain information to people involved in the hiring process those statements come with expectations. In other words, if you said you had a Harvard education, you had better be a smart person and be able to act and talk like a Harvard graduate and know all the things about the school that other Harvard grads would know. Otherwise, you stand to be discovered as a fraud.

Trying to live a lie or carry on the lie can become very difficult and stressful. It is something we should avoid at all costs. The risks far outweigh the advantages both short-term and long-term. So concentrate on getting the education and experience you need and do not lie about it.

This does not mean you cannot take what you legitimately have or earned and use words to make it sound a little bit better than it really is. Everyone does that and you should be no exception. But those "embellishments" should stop well short of lies and deceptions. Use fancy and important sounding knowledge and ply up those things you have done that pertain to the job.

But don't go so far that the embellishments turn into lies. Don't think that someone will never find out about certain things. You never know who will be talking to who or who will hire who and one day they will be talking to someone who really knows who you are and what you have done and the truth will come out. Then you can find yourself in real trouble.

Don't put anything in your resume that you cannot substantiate or that will not stand up to a serious search. Because at some time someone will search and you don't want to have to explain anything that is shown to be false. Both now and in the future.

Short-Term Jobs or Job Hopping

Some people get ahead in their careers by changing jobs frequently. This is one of the ways you can advance both in stature and in salary much faster than staying in the same company. But there are dangers in taking this approach as well and you need to balance those dangers against the benefits before you act.

Companies generally frown on people who seem to not last very long in any job they have held. Though an applicant might say they changed for a certain reason such as a new challenge, problems with a co-worker or other issue, the possibility that the applicant was actually fired often comes into people's mind. Especially if it is one short-term job after another.

Though it is much better to have a stable employment history with several long stints at each company you worked for, that does not mean that it is not possible to change jobs frequently without it being held against you. In some cases, but not all, you can explain the reasons for frequent job changes.

For example, if you can show that each job was a step up both in job responsibilities and in compensation that might suffice as a reasonable explanation for changing jobs so often. But even in that case, the reviewer might turn you down because they feel that you will just spend a short time with their company before moving on again. Since companies often spend considerable resources training new employees, they want to hire people they feel will be long-term employees.

If you do have a very short term job in your history you might want to omit it from your resume. This can be easily done if the job was only a few months by just using years in your work history and not months. This way it looks like continuous employment and even if a search reveals that other job, they really can't say you lied.

Gaps in employment can be hard to explain and you need to watch out for those when preparing your resume. Gaps indicate the loss of a job and that might be held against you.

While you don't have to explain this on a resume, you should have an answer formulated about this when you have your interview or when someone from the company calls you to discuss possible employment.

Just remember to list every job you had in the best possible way so you get the most impact from it. If you had any important responsibilities or if you have done specific things detailed in the job posting, make sure you list those specifically to draw parallels between your experience and their qualifications. In other words, like we said before, connect the dots so that anyone reading the resume will quickly realize the connections between what you have done and the job you are applying for.

Handouts &
Web-Based Information

Several years ago I applied for a position for which I thought I was well qualified for. If there was such a thing as a perfect fit between applicant and job, for me this was it. But as I constructed my resume I found I had too much relevant information and experience to fit on just a two page resume. But I needed to make sure that this information was presented to someone throughout the interview and evaluation process.

This happens to a lot of people. In fact, the longer you have been in the workforce the more information and experience you are going to have going for you. So much, at times, that you have to leave off several important entries because it would just make your resume look too long for the screener to read. So I needed to find another way.

What I came up with was a "fact sheet" that I both attached to my resume and brought with me to all the interviews I had. This "fact sheet" was targeted to the specific job as well and the sheet listed item after item where I had education or experience that would make me a better choice for the job I was interviewing for. Most of the time I was able to keep this fact sheet on one page but I guess if you were really strong, you could go two pages.

But what I thought might happen would be that the person screening the resumes would give my resume a quick once over and then, if they were interested, would go back and read through it more thoroughly. Then, after that was done they would see the fact sheet. I figured that if my resume captured their attention like I designed it to, that this fact sheet would do more of the same and really help tie things together.

Turns out I was 100% correct!

I was called in for an interview and their on the interviewer's desk was my resume and fact sheet. The resume had some notes and comments written on it which is common but the fact sheet had a lot of things circled and highlighted and there were even more notes on the fact sheet than on the resume itself! The interviewer even comments on how much he liked the fact sheet and how several items really captured his interest even though I had thought them not important enough to include on my resume.

Create your fact sheet on the same paper as your resume and send it along with your resume but to not staple or attach it. Make sure you have your name and contact information on it as well. This way if it does get separated they will know who it is for.

I have also used another method and that was not to enclose it with my resume but instead send it as a follow-up a few days after with another copy of my resume and a different cover letter drawing attention to my fact sheet. The approach here is to create name recognition by allowing the reader to see my resume twice while using the fact sheet as a reason for resending the resume. This is especially effective if you are submitted the resume to someone's e-mail address.

I also bring copies of my fact sheets to all interviews as well. In fact, I bring several in case I might be interviewing with more than one person. Copies are cheap and the more people who read about your accomplishments the better. I just hand one copy out to whoever is conducting the interview and allow them to use it as they see fit. Sometimes they don't even read it at the interview but if the interview goes well, they will definitely read it afterwards.

In this "new age" of the internet and personal websites, you might also want to create a website using your name as the domain name. This can have several benefits.

First, when they do a search under your name, which almost everyone does these days, they will see your domain at or near the top of the list. Then, on this website you create pages of information and personal details, all crafted towards getting you a job, of course, for anyone to read. Not only will the see the information you want them to see but all of that is easily sent to other people as required via a web link.

A personal website like this can also be searchable through keywords which might make your name and site show up when others are searching as well. You might even have someone contact you for a job instead of the other way around! This can be a very effective and professional way of spreading positive and impressive information about you and your career to others.

Getting personal website is easy and not at all expensive. It should cost you less than $20 to register your name and less than $5 a month to host it. You can have a professional design the site or use a template provided by some web hosts. Or, you can create your site in a content management system such as WordPress which has themes to match just about any need or design.

Whatever method you decide to use, getting more information from other sources into the hands of people you want to have it can help raise you far above anyone else applying for the job.

Remember, the people who are remembered are the people who go further. The people who do not impress are forgotten and pushed to the side. They go nowhere.

Impress people.

Be remembered.

Go somewhere.

Updating Your Resume

I'm one of those people who always say that a resume is always a work in progress. It is never finished and it is never perfected. Over time experience is added, jobs are changed, knowledge is added and performance is increased. Because of this what might have been close to a perfect resume last year might be wholly inadequate and ineffective this year.

There are two primary reasons for updating your resume at least a twice a year. Those reasons are:

First, if you go a long time without updating your resume that it will not be a matter of just tweaking your existing resume for the new opportunity but rather a complete redo of your older resume possibly taking hours. The chances of you taking the time needed to do a first rate job will depend on the urgency of the situation and you might be forced to submit less than a perfect resume when time demands.

Second, updating your resume at least twice a year enables you to easily add new things as they occur and replace older content with new and more impressive or relevant content. This helps you keep from forgetting things that might help you land that dream job you will soon be applying for. Adding things as they occur or shortly after helps insure nothing important gets lost or forgotten.

Third, as you work with resumes and become older, smarter and more experienced, you will probably find yourself more skilled at writing and creating resumes. Most of us look back at our first resume and wonder who the heck hired us based on that piece of crap! But now we can write better, express ourselves better and create better and more powerful resumes. Part of the twice yearly update is also improving wording and phrasing to make our resume more powerful and impressive.

So, let's all agree that we should update our resumes periodically. The next question should be how often should we update our resume? I would say a minimum of twice a year with an absolute, no excuses, certainly no longer time frame than once a year. Less often than that and you can count on things being lost or forgotten.

The other thing we should do as things happen in our career and life is to constantly update our list of experience and accomplishments that we hopefully made when we made our first resume.

By updating these lists almost in real time, it makes updating our resumes a breeze. We just pull up the lists, see what was added and determine whether or not the latest entries belong on our newest resume.

If you are like most people you probably will have more than one resume master file. You might have 3 or 4 depending on the jobs you applied for or the industry that you are in. Personally I would take the few minutes to update every one of those resumes. Chances are the same items will be added to each one replacing the same older entries but there will be times when there might be subtle difference and subtle changes required.

I find it useful to print out the resumes and then make notes on them as to what should be removed and what should be added. It is easier to do this on a hard copy and get an idea of how things flow than it is on a computer screen. But if you do not like to print and waste a sheet of paper you can always do your changes in the original document and save it under another name or just add the year to the end of the file.

This sometimes works great because you can always go back then and see what the original document was like before the changes.

After a while you can delete the older files as they become more and more dated. I usually keep the original plus the last 2 updated files. The files are small and will not take up a lot of room on your hard drive.

If you keep your lists current and you don't happen to have 25 different resumes on file in your computer the entire process might take you less than 2 hours or even less than an hour if not much has changed. You might even look at your resumes and see that nothing should be done based on the last few months. If that is the case, then that's fine. But make the effort to make sure every resume is accurate and current.

Printing & Sending Your Resume

Back when I entered the work force you typed your own resumes on high quality paper and sent them out. Or, you gave them to Mom or Dad to take into work and copy them on the office copier. All of that has changed now as just about everyone has a home computer and a printer. The amazing thing now is that even the cheapest home printer will produce better quality than the best copier 40 years ago! But that doesn't mean anything is good enough when it comes to printing a resume.

The first thing to consider is the paper you are going to use to print your resume on. I always recommend a higher quality paper than standard copy paper. I suggest using a "bond" type of paper that is heavier in weight and has a bit of a texture on it. This gives your resume a more professional and higher quality look and feel to it than regular white and smooth copy paper.

The second thing to consider is the color of the paper. If the job posting indicates a specific color then always give them a resume printed on that color paper. They might simply discard resumes printed on any other color paper. Sometimes people do this to see who will follow directions more closely than others. But if no specific color is stated I always liked to go with a light cream colored paper.

I like this for two reasons. First it makes it easier to find your resume in a stack of resumes printed on white paper. The second reason is that our eyes seem to notice something that is different from everything else. So a cream color resume might be noticed a bit more. I don't think this is a huge factor but anything that might work is worth a shot.

Cream color is also a conservative and professional looking color as well. While a hot pink or bright orange resume might be noticed over others it will not look professional and probably will wind up in the circular file instead of taken seriously. To be safe use a heavier pound weight paper in white or a light cream color to retain professionalism.

Now that we know what kind and color of paper to print our resume on, let's discuss the printing itself. Because if the printing is blurry or poor quality the entire resume is going to look amateurish and not be seen as professional.

Most printers today do an excellent job and should be just fine for printing a resume. But if your printer was purchased 5 years ago for $39 it might be worthwhile getting a new printer or taking your resume to a friend or print shop to get better results. Spending a couple of dollars for a professional print job will do wonders for your resume.

As far as how to send in your resume will pretty much depend on the company posting the job details. They might prefer mailing in or resumes, e-mail submission or sometimes through an on-line portal where you submit their own form instead of your personal resume. Whatever the company requires is what you should do. If they specific demands they are likely to not consider resumes received by any other means.

If you are mailing your resume to the company or to a PO Box, be sure to use a high quality envelope and make sure the name and address is written clearly and neatly. Remember that the envelope is what the person sees first and if that is messy or written in a childish scrawl that will not leave a positive impression in the eyes of the reader. If your printer has the capability to print on envelopes, strongly consider doing so. If not, consider using adhesive labels although these can give your envelop a "bulk mail" kind of feel. But that's better than seeing a messy or illegible name and address.

Address the resume as requested by the company. If you know the name of the person to send it to by all means include that on the envelope. Don't hope the resume will make it to that person, insure that it does. The same applies to the department and all other pertinent information.

Be sure to place a return address label on the envelope as well or write your return address on it. This is important because if for some reason it is not delivered it will come back to you. Then you will at least know it wasn't received and you can send out a second copy. It might be late but better late than never.

Check your resume and cover letter for quality and make sure to hand sign your cover letter as well. This gives the entire package a more personal feel instead of thinking this is just one of the 1,000 resumes you sent out this week.

Send your resume out as soon as you can. Do not rush and send an inferior resume but if you have a top notch resume ready and waiting (like you should if you followed our plan) then get it out sooner than later. The idea is to get your read earlier in the process and before the majority of resumes come in. while the reviewers will probably wait until they get a stack to go through, there is a chance that yours might be read ahead of the crunch.

This will allow the reader to spend more time reading yours than the other 1,000 they will receive next week.

As you prepare to send out your resume, let me leave you with this one important thought:

The envelope and overall quality of the envelope and resume / cover letter package is going to be the first impression the reader is going to have about you. It is your introduction to the company. Because of this you should dedicate time and effort into making this package as impressive and professional looking as possible.

Getting Professional Help

Anyone with time and home computer or access to one can create a very nice and effective resume in a few hours. However, some of us might not feel comfortable writing the text or even might not be very good at choosing the right words and phrases in order to get the maximum impact.

For those people, you can relax. There are several websites and people who will write your resume for you for a fee. There are even software programs that will help you format your resume into a professional document. Either of these resources is perfectly acceptable. In fact, simply admitting that you are not that good at these kinds of things is a huge positive for you.

That is because resumes are considered results driven documents. By that we mean a resume is considered good if it results in a serious interview. A resume might look great and sound great but if you send 100 of those resumes out and don't get a single call back then you are either going after the wrong jobs or the resumes is not a very good one.

Because so much rides on the effectiveness of your resume, it is better to pay a professional to create a great resume for you than to try and do it yourself and not go anywhere. It is time and money very well spent.

But if you are going get professional assistance with your resume consider one very important thing:

Your resume is only going to be as good as the information you provide the writer. IN other words, if you don't give them all the right information they will not be able to write the best resume for you. So get your monies worth and spend some time gathering information so that they can do their magic and create a great resume for you.

The great thing about getting professional assistance with your resume is that once you get it you can work off that copy from that point on and make changes to the existing framework. So you pay once and then work in your changes from that point on. It's a pretty effective formula for success.

While this will also save you time you need to plan a bit in advance when you hire someone else to work for you. You cannot call them up Monday night and tell them you need a resume for Tuesday afternoon! Even if they could work that kind of magic the overall quality would be less than if they had the time to really work on a resume for you. If this is your intention, make sure you get the documents on a flash drive or in an e-mail so you can open them with your word processor. Getting a paper document would mean you would have to manually transcribe and format everything yourself which kind of defeats the entire process.

Some resume writers will charge by the resume or by the page so decide which is better for you and get a price in advance. Also decide whether you would like them to write your cover letter for you as well. Again, you can have them write one and then do a cut and paste changing the words around for future letters you might use later on. Other might charge by the word or have an established package price including resume, cover letter and pre-printed envelope as well. If that is the case all you need to do is hand sign the cover letter and mail it away. But again, you will need to give them time to prepare the documents for you.

If you do decide to get professional assistance, ask to see some samples of the persons work or even better, get a personal recommendation from someone you trust so you can have a good and secure feeling going into the   process.

Keep a List of Resumes Sent

For some of us, we send out or submit just one or two resumes when promotions come up or opportunities are being searched for. But for others, they might send out 50 or 100 resumes as they try to gain employment or seek a bigger or better job. For these people it is probably a good idea to create a list of the resumes that we sent out and where the opportunity came from.

Some companies will submit the same job posting to different websites or newspapers at different times. For example they might post a job on one site and then when they did not get any good applicants, they try another site or another type of media. Keeping track of where you sent resumes will allow you to recognize where you already sent resumes to in the past.

There are two viewpoints when it comes to resubmitting resumes for the same opportunity advertised in two different time frames. One says if you resume was not considered good enough the first time why bother submitting it again. The other view is that what do you have to lose except for a few minutes time, a couple of sheets or paper and a stamp?

I look at it this way:

If it is a job you really wanted the second posting might be looked at as good news because it means no one has been hired for it as yet. This means you have a second chance to fine-tune your resume and cover letter and make it more powerful and more impressive. There is also a chance that they originally set their sights too high or expected too much and now they have lowered their requirements a bit. So what might not have impressed them in the beginning could very well impress them now.

If you find you have already submitted a resume for a job you were really interested in, there is nothing that says you cannot send it in again. Unless the resumes were entered into a computer somehow they might never even realize that you had sent them in before. You in essence you get a second shot at a job you really want. You should not get discouraged that you didn't make it the first time. Consider the second chance a new opportunity and see how you can better impress the same people the second time around.

The other reason for keeping track of resumes sent is that you can follow-up with these companies in a couple of week to see if there is anything else you can do to help them with the hiring process. Maybe send a follow-up letter with another resume or a new or different fact sheet designed to further enhance your qualifications for the position.

These follow-ups are sometimes successful for two reasons.

First of all sometimes resumes do get lost in the mail or delivered to the wrong person or just get lost in the shuffle as hundreds, possibly thousands of resumes all come in for the same position. The end result is that you might be the perfect person for the job but no one ever sees your resume or knows about you. This has happened and who knows how many people lost out on their dream job because of a lost resume.

Second, by you sending a resume in at a later date you might get someone to read it without the pressure of a stack of other resumes staring at them on their desk. This means that sometimes your resume might get a bit more time and attention. Or, it could get trashed because it came in late. But if there are no great slam dunk candidates then your resume might get a second life.

One last reason to keep track of where you sent resumes is that you might get a call from someone months later and have no idea who that person is, what she is calling about and which particular job you applied for. There is no way you can BS your way through that conversation without coming off looking like a fool. But if you can do a quick check before you call the person back, or even while you are talking to them, it will soon be crystal clear about what they are calling about. Then you can talk intelligently and further your case instead of looking like someone who really didn't care much about the opportunity in the first place.

Regardless of the reason you might have, it just makes sense to understand who you sent resumes out to, what the particular job you applied for, and when you sent in the resume. This is the only way you can keep track of what you did and know what you are going to do moving forward.

Conclusion

Over the years resume design and creation has changed considerably. We now have computers and printers that have all but made the typewriter obsolete. What used to take specialized skills and equipment can now be done by anyone in the privacy of their own home.

But despite this there are still lazy people who look to do as little as possible and still get the results that they want. If you are not one of those people then you should be thankful for them. Because every person that looks for the shortcuts and looks for the easy way out makes it that much easier for you to get the jobs that you want.

One of the things I learned early on in life is that there are always going to be people who absolutely refuse to do the very things that can make them successful. These aren't always the most difficult or hardest tasks.

But the tasks that appear to mean little often add up to make a huge difference and this is what you need to understand about resume design and career building.

It is up to you right now to decide if you are going to be the one who takes the short cuts and looks for the easy way out or are you going to be the one who does all the little things that are needed to be successful. It's you choice to make and it's up to you to make the choice and live with the results of those choices.

This entire process is not difficult and it is not time consuming either. It requires no special skills other than a "so-so" talent for writing and that you can easily get help with. It won't take a lot of effort and it won't take a ton of time either if you follow the suggestions in this book. But it is going to take some effort.

Sometimes I laugh when someone says they are not lucky or that someone else has all the luck. For me personally, I believe we make our own luck. We become successful because we are willing to do what is needed to be successful. We get opportunities because we are ready for them when they arrive. We get the breaks because we paved the way for them weeks, months and years before hand.

It is easy to blame our lack of success or progress on luck or chance but the reality is the things we do or don't do usually make all the difference in the world. Yes, some people just happen to be in the right place at the right time and opportunity knocks for them when that happens.

But even when that does happen to someone remember this: They have to be prepared and ready even when that happens or that opportunity will pass them by.

"Resume Hacks" will get you started by showing you how to create an engaging, impressive and totally professional looking resume. That is step one. When your resume is successful the next step will be the interviews that will follow. Hopefully before that comes you will grab a copy of "Interview Hacks" which will do for interviews pretty much the same thing this book did for resumes. It will give you everything you need in one place to prepare you to ace any interview you might find yourself in.

But no matter which books you buy and which ones you read, it all comes down to you. What you are willing to do and what you are not willing to do. You make the decisions and you deal with the consequences. There is a world of opportunity and great jobs out there. You just have to put yourself in the right position to take advantage of them when they come.

So do the right thing and start preparing yourself today for what might come tomorrow. Give yourself the time to create a powerful, engaging and professional looking resume today so you will have it when you need it.

Amazing things happen to people who prepare themselves for them before they arrive. Become one of those people. Start your new resume today!

Bonus Content!

Most Common Resume Mistakes

Sometimes we all do things that we shouldn't do and we do those things without thinking. It's not that we want to hurt ourselves or spoil our chances, it is just that we are not aware of how much certain little things can impact the results we get.

Because of this, it is important to be aware of what NOT to do as well as the things that we should be doing. Here is a list of the common mistakes people often make when creating and sending out their resumes. Just keep these in mind as you start preparing your own resume. They just might help make the difference between no call and an interview!

Typos & Mistakes

Remember that your resume is a look into who you are and how well you function. It is also an insight into the quality of work you produce and your level of professionalism. If your resume contains misspelled words or poor grammar, the reader is not likely to be very impressed with you. ALWAYS proof read your resume before printing it and again before sending it out.

Check for spelling and read it to check for proper flow. One trick to capture spelling mistakes is to read the resume backwards. This makes your brain look at each individual word instead of reading the flow which might make you skip over some words because the brain knows what's coming.

Another helpful tip is to have someone else read it for you. Another set of eyes might pick up one or two things your eyes just missed. The person might also have suggestions about which words to use and how to better help with the overall flow. Someone in the same type of position you are applying for might really be a help as they might be aware of certain things your resume should include as far as that specific position is concerned. It's a little thing but we all know by now how a little thing can make a huge difference at times!

Poorly Written

Writing is a skill that is developed over time.

Many people cannot write very well and it is not because they lack the skill or ability. It is because they don't practice it or apply it often enough. Your first resume is not likely to be a great one. But as you create another resume and another after that, your eyes and brain will learn and you will see your end product becoming better and better.

A poorly written resume is a poor reflection of who you are and what kind of work you can do. Even if the job you are applying for does not require writing skills, those writing skills are what you have to do in order to impress someone enough to want to get to know more about you.

So take the time to create a great resume. Make 5 or 6 drafts of it and you will notice each one getting a little bit better as you learn. Ask for help if you need it. Remember this is a results driven document. If it doesn't result in a call back or an interview it didn't do its job well enough. Just keep practicing and tweaking until you know it's good enough to send out.

Then tweak it some more because "good enough" usually isn't good enough to land an interview let alone a great job!

Too Short

This one is easy. If your resume is too short it will either leave out important information or give the reader the perception that you have very little to offer.

Neither one of those things are good to have in the mind of the reader. Make sure you have enough good and high quality content to fill up at least one page. If you don't have it, find a way to get it. Attend a class or seminar and add that to your education. Ask for more responsibilities at your current job so you can add them to your resume. In short, do what you have to do to make your resume look full and impressive.

You can also try things like adding a little bit more white space or increasing the size of the fonts you used. But keep in mind that you can only do this a little bit before the resume starts to look awkward and phony or fake. If you are a line or two short these things might work. If you are only at a half a page, they won't. If that's your resume go out and get more experience or find more things to add to it.

Too Long

On the flip side, if your resume is bordering on the great American novel, chances are nobody is going to sit down and read it. They just do not have the time. They might try and skim through it but it is more likely it will get tossed aside or in the trash and never be read. So we really need to remove some content or shorten the wording to get the resume back down to the two page maximum.

Start removing the content that is the least impressive or relevant. This sometimes is all that needs to be done and the result is that you have two pages filled with high quality and impressive content instead of 5 pages with a lot of garbage mixed in.

Resumes are a perfect example that less is often more. Start with the great content to capture the attention of the reader and keep great content coming to keep them reading. That is how you create a successful and engaging resume!

If you really do have 4 or 5 pages of highly impressive and top quality content, you still don't want your resume to be that long. Put the best of the best in your resume and consider using a fact sheet for the rest. Using that approach will increase the chances of your resume actually being read.

Too General

Your resume needs to be specific and targeted and it must resonate with the person reading it. When someone reads your resume they need to be able to picture you succeeding in the position you are applying for. They need to see your experience and education as they pertain to that specific job. If they don't see those connections you could miss out on a lot of opportunities.

Choose your content and wording so it is as specific to the job as possible. Create different resumes for each job you apply for so that each resume is powerful and impressive. You simply cannot use a "one size fits all" generic resume and expect to get any kind of positive results. Those resumes sometimes don't even work for the lowest quality or level jobs. They surely are not going to work for the higher paying and more selective opportunities.

The same applies to your cover letter as well. Take the time to write a customized cover letter specifically for the job you are applying for. Connect posted qualifications with what you have to offer so the reader immediately sees the connection between you and the position. Don't leave anything to chance in either your resume or cover letter. Other applicants won't so you had better not either!

Too Jammed Packed or Difficult to Read

The easier it is for someone to do something the more likely it is that they will actually do it. This also applies to reading resumes. If your resume is clear and easy to read, the reader is more likely to read further and perhaps even the entire resume.

But if you print it in #6 font and jam 4 pages of material into two chocked full pages, they are more likely to give up and toss it away and move on to the next one. Also remember that it is possible that the person trying to red your resume might not have perfect vision and if they have to squint and strain to try and read your resume, it will just get tossed.

Make the font size easy to read but not so large that it looks phony or awkward. Leave plenty of white space so the eye finds what it is looking for easily. Make it flow well so it is easy and enjoyable to read and make the reader want to read more. But if they cannot read it easily to begin with, you have a problem.

Poor Objective

Everyone looking for a job is "looking for a job in the engineering field where I can excel and have the opportunity to advance". So don't use that kind of generic garbage in your objective. Your objective is one of the first things the person sees when they start reading your resume. If that doesn't capture their information, or if the entry is a boring piece of crap, they might stop and go no further!

Your objective, like the rest of the resume needs to be targeted directly to the job you are applying for working in a bit of your personal education or experience into it to start generating a positive impression. Something like "Mechanical Engineer with Advanced Degrees and 15 years professional experience seeks Project Manager position with a large Northeastern Defense Company"

Isn't that a much more targeted and powerful statement? It showcases both your education and experience as well as connects it to the exact job you are applying for. A person reading that is going to be excited and will eagerly want to keep reading for more information about you!

Incorrect Contact Information

This is more common than you might think but be sure to carefully proof read your contact information.

If your phone number is off my just one digit, they cannot call you. If your e-mail has 2 letters switched, they cannot e-mail you. If your address is off for some reason they will not be able to contact you by mail. All of these things should be carefully checked and proof read so you know they are accurate.

Do not think people will spend the time to research your information to find the correct versions. They will make a call and if they get a wrong number they will try again. If you wrote down the wrong number they will more likely just move on to someone else! No one has the time to tack down the correct information and contact you.

If you enjoyed "Resume Hacks" and would like to go even further in the hiring process and get even better results, why not check out these related "Hacks" titles?

Career Hacks

Interview Hacks

Also Available Where You Purchased this Book!